LEGENDS OF WARFARE
AVIATION

F-104 Starfighter
Lockheed's Sleek Cold War Interceptor

DAVID DOYLE

SCHIFFER MILITARY

4880 Lower Valley Road   Atglen, PA 19310

1

Designed by Christopher Bower
Cover design by Justin Watkinson
Type set in Impact/Minion Pro/Univers LT Std

ISBN: 978-0-7643-6786-1
Printed in India

Published by Schiffer Publishing, Ltd.
4880 Lower Valley Road
Atglen, PA 19310
Phone: (610) 593-1777; Fax: (610) 593-2002
Email: Info@schifferbooks.com
Web: www.schifferbooks.com

For our complete selection of fine books on this and related subjects, please visit our website at www.schifferbooks.com. You may also write for a free catalog.

Schiffer Publishing's titles are available at special discounts for bulk purchases for sales promotions or premiums. Special editions, including personalized covers, corporate imprints, and excerpts, can be created in large quantities for special needs. For more information, contact the publisher.

We are always looking for people to write books on new and related subjects. If you have an idea for a book, please contact us at proposals@schifferbooks.com.

Acknowledgments

This book would not have been possible without the generous help of many friends, including Tom Kailbourn, Scott Taylor, Dana Bell, David Dwight Jackson, Hans-Heiri Stapfer, the staff at the San Diego Air and Space Museum, Brett Stolle at the National Museum of the United States Air Force, the staff of the National Archives, the late Massimio Foti, and, of course, my wonderful wife, Denise.

All photos are courtesy of the National Museum of the United States Air Force unless otherwise noted. Illustrations by Vincenzo Auletta.

Contents

Introduction 004

CHAPTER 1 The First Starfighter: XF-104 006

CHAPTER 2 Service Test and Production Prototypes: YF-104 014

CHAPTER 3 The Starfighter Enters Service: F-104A 022

CHAPTER 4 The Two-Seater Starfighter: F-104B 052

CHAPTER 5 More Power: F-104C and D 060

CHAPTER 6 The Starfighter for Everyone: F-104G 091

CHAPTER 7 NASA Gets Its Own Starfighters: F-104N 126

CHAPTER 8 The Canadian Starfighter: CF-104 130

CHAPTER 9 Built in Japan: F-104J 136

CHAPTER 10 The Ultimate Starfighter: F-104S 140

Introduction

US pilots flying over Korea in 1950 encountered a new—and highly effective—aircraft, the Mikoyan-Gurevich MiG-15 fighter. Encountering the swept-wing fighter was a surprise to the US pilots, and decades later a further surprise would be revealed when it was learned that many of those MiGs were flown not by North Korean or Chinese pilots but, rather, Soviet pilots. This led to the air superiority over Korea being bitterly contested between US pilots flying the F-86 Sabre and Communist pilots in the MiG-15. The MiG-15 exceeded the Sabre in zoom climb, rate of climb, ceiling, acceleration, and speed. The robust F-86 could outdive the MiG, and since many of the Sabre pilots were experienced World War II combat veterans, the dive ability gave them an edge against North Korean and Chinese pilots. However, as already stated, many suspected—and it has since been confirmed—that most early-war MiGs were flown by Soviet pilots. The Soviet pilots were also World War II combat veterans.

The result was losses that were unacceptable to the USAF, and a demand from pilots in theater for an aircraft that would best the MiG-15.

Such was the concern about the capabilities of the MiG-15 that the United States launched a plan dubbed Operation Moolah, which offered $50,000 to any pilot to deliver a fully mission-capable MiG-15 to United Nations forces. Included in the offer was political asylum, resettlement in a non-Communist country, and anonymity if desired. It would be September 1953, two months after the end of the Korean War, before North Korean lieutenant No Kum-Sok would defect with a MiG-15. He was unaware of the reward.

Back in December 1951, the USAF invited several luminaries from the US aviation industry to Korea to discuss with pilots their needs and desires in future generations of fighters. Among the industry leaders who participated in the discussions was Lockheed's Clarence "Kelly" Johnson.

Upon his return to the United States, Johnson put together a team and set out to design a fighter that could fly higher and faster than any adversary. Lockheed management approved the design on October 31, 1952. Shortly thereafter, Johnson and his team presented Lockheed's Project L-246, or Model 83, to the Air Force at Wright Field.

The Air Force liked what they saw, drew up a General Operating Requirement for a similar aircraft, and solicited responses from industry. North American, Northrop, and Republic responded along with Lockheed. Not surprisingly, Lockheed had the most refined proposal.

The Lockheed Model 83 drew upon the company's experience with the X-7 ramjet test vehicle as well as the Douglas X-3 Stiletto design. A key component of the design was the ultrathin, low-aspect-ratio wing. The leading-edge radius was only 0.016 inches—which meant that, once the aircraft was produced, scabbards would be used to protect the ground crews from injury on the sharp edge of the wing.

On March 1, 1953, a contract was issued for the production of two prototypes under Weapon System 303A (WS-303A), to be designated XF-104. Lockheed anticipated this outcome and used its own money to begin work on the project. This initiative resulted in the first flight of XF-104 on March 4, 1954—only one year and three days after the contract was signed.

When war broke out in Korea, the F-86 Sabre was America's frontline fighter. While it was well armed and robust, Sabre pilots found themselves outdistanced by pilots of opposing MiG-15 fighters. Pilots demanded an aircraft with better performance. *National Archives*

The relatively lightweight MiG-15 flown by North Korean defector No Kum-Sok is parked at a US airbase. Faster than the Sabre, the MiG was a potent adversary. It was especially dangerous when flown by Soviet pilots—as happened clandestinely in North Korea.

CHAPTER 1
The First Starfighter: XF-104

The first XF-104, as well as the second, certainly looked, while at a distance, like the thousands of successors, but in truth the two XF-104 prototypes were very different. These aircraft were powered by the Buick-built Wright J65 turbojet, a licensed copy of the Armstrong Siddeley Sapphire.

The J65 was substantially smaller than the General Electric J79 engine that was used in the production F-104 aircraft, and accordingly the XF-104s were more than 5 feet shorter in length than later Starfighters.

Assembly of the first XF-104, serial number 53-7786, was conducted in secret. Once completed, on February 24, 1954, it was trucked under cover of night from Lockheed's Burbank plant to Edwards Air Force Base. Taxi tests of 53-7786 began on February 27, 1954. High-speed taxi tests, which included a short hop about 5 feet off the ground, occurred the next day. On March 4, 1954, Lockheed test pilot A. W. "Tony" LeVier took the aircraft up for its first flight.

However, a malfunction prevented the landing gear from retracting. Accordingly, the flight was both brief and slow.

Even with the landing-gear issues corrected, the XF-104 could not exceed the speed of sound in level flight. The J65-B-3 simply did not have enough power. When the aircraft was put in a slight descent, Mach 1 could be exceeded and no problems were encountered. In July 1954, the J65-W-7 was installed. It was a more powerful engine equipped with an afterburner. This gave the XF-104 a Mach 1.49 top speed in level flight at 41,000 feet.

The second prototype, serial number 53-7787, was equipped with the afterburner-equipped J65-W-7 engine from the outset. On March 25, 1955, Lockheed test pilot Ray Goudey pushed the second prototype up to Mach 1.79, the fastest speed ever achieved by an XF-104.

Armed with the experimental T171 Gatling-type cannon, the second prototype was intended to serve as the armament test bed. However, about three weeks after the record-seeking flight, the aircraft was lost while on a test flight. Lockheed pilot Herman "Fish" Salmon was conducting an in-flight firing test when the cockpit suffered an explosive decompression. It was misdiagnosed as a gun malfunction, and Salmon ejected using the downward-firing ejection seat.

The flight-testing program soldiered on with the single, initial prototype until it was joined by the YF-104A in February 1956. By that time the XF-104 had accumulated 250 hours.

The first prototype XF-104, USAF serial number 53-7786, flies over the desert in early 1954. In response to the challenge posed by the Soviet-manufactured jet fighters in the early days of the Korean War, Lockheed Aircraft—on its own initiative—drafted a design proposal for a high-speed, high-altitude interceptor to defeat current and future Soviet aircraft. The Air Force accepted the proposal and issued Lockheed a contract for two prototypes designated XF-104 in March 1953.

The XF-104 stabilator (a horizontal tail that combines the stabilizer and elevator) is mounted atop the dorsal fin to prevent inertia coupling. Inertia coupling is a condition in which the inertia of the fuselage defeats the aerodynamic stabilizing forces of the wings and the empennage during high-speed flight. *National Archives*

The first prototype XF-104 parks on Rogers Dry Lake during flight tests at the Air Force Flight Test Center, Edwards Air Force Base, California, on July 22, 1954. Below the tail number is printed "LOCKHEED" and the company's winged-star logo. The lines of the XF-104s were generally similar to those of the production F-104s. The most noticeable difference was the shorter fuselage of the XF-104. Additionally, the air inlets of the XF-104 had a different shape than the F-104. *National Archives*

The wings of the XF-104s were very short and were the thinnest ever used on a production aircraft. The wings had a pronounced negative dihedral of –10 degrees. This counterbalanced the overly stabilizing effect of the empennage, especially in rolling turns. *National Archives*

The first XF-104 rolls forward on Rogers Dry Lake at Edwards Air Force Base during tests on July 22, 1954. The Lockheed logo was also present to the front of the buzz number. Instead of XF-104, the buzz number included the prefix FG and the last three digits of the tail number.

The wing area of the first XF-104 is relatively small, and the length of the fuselage is 2.5 times as long as the wingspan. Detachable wingtip fuel tanks of 170 gallons each were developed for the XF-104 and production planes. These tanks extended the ferry and combat ranges of the aircraft without the expense of additional internal fuel tanks and the consequent larger fuselage size.

The first XF-104 flies over California farmland in 1954. Sometimes described as an engine with a pair of wings, the Lockheed F-104 was designed by famous engineer Kelly Johnson and his team. From the XF-104 through the F-104S, the final model, 2,578 examples were produced by numerous manufacturers. *NARA*

The first XF-104 flies over Southern California farmlands on a test flight. Power was supplied by the Wright XJ65 jet engine. On production F-104s, this engine would be replaced by the General Electric J79 axial-flow turbojet engine.

The two XF-104s fly in formation together. USAF serial number 53-7787 with buzz number FG-787, the second prototype, is in the foreground, while the first prototype is in the background. The Lockheed logo seen previously was replaced by "LOCKHEED" in larger block letters. *National Archives*

The Century Series planes, *from top to bottom*, are McDonnell F-101 Voodoo, Convair F-102 Delta Dagger, North American F-100 Super Sabre, and the first Lockheed XF-104 Starfighter. The Century Series were USAF fighter jets with model numbers in the 100 range; they included only interceptors and fighter-bombers. These planes were built for high performance and featured advanced avionics. The F-101 Voodoo was the first aircraft in the USAF inventory that could exceed a speed of 1,000 miles per hour. The F-102 was the world's first aircraft to use Whitcomb area rule in its design to reduce drag.

Three Century Series jets, the F-101, F-102, and F-106, were equipped to fire air-to-air nuclear missiles for defense against enemy bombers. While guided missiles were under development, USAF officials hypothesized that a single nuclear-armed missile could simultaneously eliminate several massed Soviet bombers with nuclear payloads. The Douglas AIR-2 Genie had a 1.5-kiloton W25 nuclear warhead that could create a 300-meter (1,000 foot) blast radius. From 1957 to 1963, a total of 3,150 nuclear rounds were produced with the MB-1 designation to be fired by these interceptors at Soviet bomber formations.

CHAPTER 2
Service Test and Production Prototypes: YF-104

Lockheed's 17 YF-104As were considered production-prototype aircraft leading to the F-104A. This understanding allowed both the Air Force and manufacturer to make modest design improvements as they got feedback from the field. The YF-104s were expected to function at full production standards after the service test period. F-104 development and procurement were handled similarly to aircraft purchased prior to World War II. The experimental, or XF-model, aircraft would be followed by a group of service test aircraft, or YF series, prior to full-scale series production.

Following this pattern, the Air Force ordered a group of seventeen YF-104A aircraft in July 1954, and the type made its first flight on February 17, 1956. The Air Force began accepting the aircraft later that month. These aircraft differed from the experimental XF-104 in that they were initially outfitted with General Electric XJ79-GE-3 turbojet engines, which generated 14,800 pounds of thrust with afterburner. The new engine required

the aircraft to be 5 feet, 6 inches longer than the XF-104 to accommodate the larger engine. The engine also required a modification to the air intake design, which included half cones. The air intake design was subject to considerable secrecy. The intakes featured covered fairings during publicity photos to completely obscure the design. The XJ79 engines were later replaced by full-production J79-GE-3A engines.

The YF-104 featured a forward-retracting front landing gear and two additional fuel cells in the fuselage.

Despite some initial problems, the XJ79 engine enabled YF-104A 55-2955 to reach Mach 2 on February 28, 1956. It was the first fighter to double the speed of sound in level flight. YF-104As also captured a world altitude record of 91,249 feet on May 7, 1958, when Maj. Howard C. Johnson was at the controls. Nine days later, a world airspeed record of 1,404.19 mph was set by the hands of Capt. Walter W. Irwin.

After the order for the two XF-104 prototypes, the US Air Force issued a contract to Lockheed for seventeen YF-104As. These were considered service-test or production-prototype aircraft, preceding the first production model, the F-104A. The most significant visual difference between the YF-104A and the XF-104 was the longer fuselage of the YF-104. At 54.7 feet, the YF-104A was 5.6 feet longer than the XF-104. The longer General Electric J79-GE-3 turbojet engine was used in the YF-104A and added length.

The first YF-104A, USAF serial number 55-2955, taxies down a runway. The uncovered right engine air inlet is visible on this aircraft.

The second YF-104A, USAF serial number 55-2956, has an aluminum-alloy cover installed over the inlet. The cover was a security measure undertaken early on to hide the shape of the inlets from prying eyes. These inlets varied from those of the XF-104 because conical ramps, also called shock cones, jut from their fronts. The ramps served to create the optimal ram effect at speeds faster than Mach 1.5.

The second YF-104A rolls out of Lockheed's Palmdale, California, plant on April 17, 1956. These and subsequent F-104s underwent final assembly at the Palmdale plant. Intake covers are installed, and a version of the Lockheed logo is on the vertical tail and the nose. *National Archives*

The second YF-104A, 55-2956, undertakes its official rollout. Wing tanks were not installed at this time. An air-data probe projects from the nose. These probes were used during flight tests to measure air pressure, angle of attack, and sideslip. *National Archives*

Afterburners roar as the 11th YF-104A, USAF serial number 55-2965, undergoes ground tests of the engine at Edwards Air Force Base around June 1957. The ventral fin feature was introduced during F-104A production and retrofitted to YF-104As. *National Archives*

This YF-104A, with USAF serial number 55-2966, displays its right wingtip tank on October 17, 1957. Numerous stencils are present on the tank. During flight tests, flutter was experienced due to instability of the wingtip tanks. Consequently, various designs of fins were tested on the tanks. *National Archives*

YF-104A, USAF serial number 55-2956, has officially rolled out of Lockheed's Palmdale plant in February 1956. The contoured aluminum-alloy covers over the inlets appear from a distance to be an integral part of the fuselage, but they were designed to be removed after the aircraft was initially unveiled to the public. The pronounced fairing along the spine of the fuselage was a feature not present on the XF-104. The fuselage spine would continue on production F-104s.

YF-104A, USAF serial number 55-2963, is marked "PHASE 5"—a reference to a test phase. On the side of the fuselage above the nose gear door is a bulged fairing. The bulge was designed to replicate the fairing on future F-104s armed with the M61 Vulcan 20 mm gun.

YF-104A, USAF serial number 55-2971, flipped over and was severely damaged while engaged in arrester-barrier tests at Edwards Air Force Base in early October 1958. The pilot survived the crash, and the plane was repaired and eventually returned to service. *National Archives*

The nose gear doors are open, but the main-gear doors are closed on the fifth YF-104A. The outlines of the main-gear doors are visible between the national insignia on the wing and the fuselage of USAF serial number 55-2959. The landing gear was hydraulically operated. The nose gear and the main gear retracted forward, while the main gear also rotated as it retracted or extended to enable it to fit into the fuselage. Variations are visible on the metal panels of the wings, fuselage, and exhaust areas. *National Archives*

CHAPTER 3
The Starfighter Enters Service: F-104A

Drawing from YF-104A experiences, several improvements were incorporated into the production F-104A. Most significant was the strengthened airframe—capable of withstanding 7.33 g operation. An aft-mounted ventral fin improved directional stability especially at high altitudes and speeds. A boundary layer control system was also added.

While the F-104A had been ordered for Tactical Air Command (TAC), circumstances dictated aircraft delivery to the Air Defense Command (ADC) instead.

The F-104A was a day fighter rather than an all-weather interceptor. The AN/ASG-14T-1 fire control system was insufficient to intercept the enemy at night or during low visibility.

TAC lost interest due to the modest offensive armament capability and low endurance of the Starfighter. Although disappointed by the F-104A's endurance and limited visibility, ADC took the Starfighters because delivery of F-106 Delta Darts was delayed. The Starfighter redeemed itself with an impressive rate of climb and Mach 2 capability.

The Air Force initially ordered 146 of the F-104As. Later orders pushed this to a planned 722 aircraft. However, TAC's loss of interest as well as funding shortages resulted in only 153 F-104As. The final F-104A was delivered in December 1958.

The aircraft were to be armed with the M61 Vulcan cannon and wingtip-mounted Sidewinder missiles. However, YF-104A tests revealed problems with M61. The Air Force ordered that the cannon no longer be installed during F-104A production on November 1, 1957. The order included the Vulcan's removal from previously produced aircraft.

It would be a year before the Vulcan problems related to the high g-forces applied to the weapon were corrected. The resulting improved gun, the M61A1, was retrofitted to the Starfighters in 1964.

Also problematic were the J79-GE-3 and later J79-GE-3A engines found in the F-104A. These engines proved to be prone to flameouts, oil loss, and ignition failures, resulting in the grounding of the F-104As in April 1958. This was largely resolved through the installation of the J79-GE-3B, which was more reliable and produced 9,600 pounds dry thrust or 14,800 pounds thrust with afterburner.

Originally equipped, like the previous Starfighters, with downward-firing ejection seats, in service these were replaced with Lockheed C-2 upward-firing seats. Additional modifications made to the aircraft while in service included the installation of a ventral fin beneath the fuselage and boundary layer control added to the flaps.

The F-104A first became operational on February 20, 1958, with the 83rd Fighter-Interceptor Squadron (FIS) at Hamilton Air Force Base (AFB) in California. In succession, the F-104A was fielded next by the 56th FIS at Wright-Patterson AFB in Ohio, the 337th FIS at Westover AFB in Massachusetts, and the 538th FIS at Larson AFB in Washington.

F-104A-10-LO, USAF serial number 56-0758, features wingtip fuel tanks as it awaits a mission. The F-104A was the first production model of the Starfighter. A total of 153 examples were delivered. Six were production-standard planes, and the balance were delivered to Tactical Air Command and the Air Defense Command. The F-104As were similar in appearance to the YF-104As and initially were powered by the same General Electric J79-GE-3 or -3A turbojet engines. However, these turbojet engines proved unreliable and were soon replaced with the J79-GE-3B turbojet engine.

The sleek contours of the F-104A are especially evident when viewed from the front of the nose. The position of the pitot tube on the front of the radome necessitated considerable engineering and problem-solving to enable the radar to "see" past the obstruction of the pitot tube.

Lockheed F-104A-10-LO (LO designates a Lockheed aircraft built in Burbank), USAF serial number 56-0758, exhibits a highly polished fuselage. The F-104A was constructed in seven main production blocks, numbered 1, 5, 10, 15, 20, 25, and 30. The number of the production block appeared as the first suffix in the aircraft's nomenclature designation; thus, the number 10 in this plane's designation. The second suffix, LO, stood for Lockheed. This plane is fitted with an air-data probe painted in red and white rings.

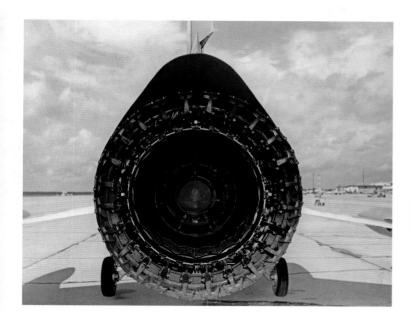

From the rear of an F-104A, the interior of the J79 engine nozzle is visible. The original J79-GE-3 and -3A engines proved so unreliable that all F-104As were grounded in April 1958. Once the more reliable J79-GE-3Bs were installed, the F-104As were returned to service.

A rail-mounted Sidewinder infrared-homing missile is mounted on the wingtip of an F-104A in September 1957. Sidewinders were used for air-to-air combat missions that did not require wingtip tanks. The US Navy–developed Sidewinder entered service in 1956.

Lockheed F-104A-5-LO, USAF serial number 56-0737, banks left during a flight over the desert. This Starfighter was the first of eleven examples of the F-104A-5-LO. A GAR-8 (later designated AIM-9) Sidewinder air-to-air missile is mounted on each wingtip. The ventral fin on this aircraft was painted in a dark color. The outline of the right main landing-gear door is clearly visible. The buzz number FG-737 is marked on the rear part of the fuselage.

F-104A-15-LO 56-0772 is parked on a hardstand at the Air Force Flight Test Center at Edwards Air Force Base in California on January 3, 1958. The Starfighter rests without a standard wingtip fuel tank or a GAR-8 Sidewinder missile. *National Archives*

The third production F-104A-15-LO, USAF serial number 56-0766, features a Philco-manufactured GAR-8 Sidewinder missile installed on the wingtip. This air-to-air missile had a 10-pound warhead, triggered by an infrared proximity or contact fuse. *National Archives*

Two Sidewinder-armed F-104A-15-LOs escort a Lockheed EC-121 Warning Star early-warning and control aircraft—a 1950s precursor of present-day AWACS aircraft. The Starfighter to the left is USAF serial number 56-0769, while the one to the right is 56-0781.

Technicians inspect "Vociferous Viking," F-104A-20-LO 56-0791, at Taoyuan Air Base in Taiwan on September 19, 1958. Douglas C-124s airlifted this and other Starfighters of the 83rd Fighter-Interceptor Squadron to help bolster the defenses of the island.

During a long-distance flight, F-104A-10-LO 56-0761 carries both wingtip fuel tanks and drop tanks on wing pylons. The refueling probe is extended and visible to the front left of the windscreen. The probe came in the form of a kit that was easily installed or removed. With the tip of the probe in proximity to the pilot, it was possible for the pilot to watch the approach to the refueling drogue while he enjoyed a clear view to the front of the plane.

Lt. Col. Raymond E. Evans, commander of the 83rd Fighter-Interceptor Squadron, is clad in an MC-4 high-altitude partial-pressure suit in February 1958. For high-altitude flights, F-104 pilots must wear a pressure suit to prevent oxygen deprivation.

**YF-104A
(Early)**

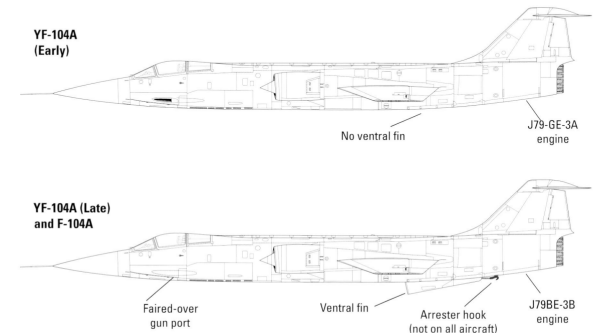

No ventral fin

J79-GE-3A engine

**YF-104A (Late)
and F-104A**

Faired-over gun port

Ventral fin

Arrester hook (not on all aircraft)

J79BE-3B engine

Visible differences between the early YF-104A and the late YF-104A are illustrated in these diagrams. The late YF-104A introduced a ventral fin to increase stability. In addition, the gunport was faired over on the late YF-104A.

The fifth F-104A-1-LO, USAF serial number 56-0734, bears the marking "NASA" in black block letters on a yellow stripe with thin black borders on the dorsal fin. The radome is a matte black, the antiglare panel to the front of the windscreen is matte dark green, while the pilot's headrest is red. The wings are black, with white flaps and ailerons. No pitot tube is present on the tip of the radome, but an air-data probe is present on the left wingtip. *NASA*

Lockheed F-104A-25-LO, USAF serial number 56-0844, bears markings of the South Carolina Air National Guard. This aircraft was assigned to the 157th Fighter-Interceptor Squadron of the 169th Fighter-Interceptor Group, South Carolina Air National Guard.

The pilot of F-104A-25-LO, USAF serial number 56-0842, is in the cockpit during a deployment to Taoyuan Air Base in Taiwan. Starfighters were dispatched to Taiwan in September 1958, in a show of strength against China during the Quemoy-Matsu Crisis.

Lockheed F-104As of the 56th Fighter-Interceptor Squadron line up on a hardstand at Wright-Patterson Air Force Base in the fall of 1959. The squadron insignia is on the tails of these planes. All aircraft are either F-104A-25s or F-104A-30s.

F-104A-10-LO 56-0755 features an interesting paint scheme. The top of the fuselage is natural metal, while the lower surfaces are painted a light color, with a black border between the paint and natural metal. The wings and vertical tail are a light color with numerous touch-ups. The aircraft's 0-prefix serial number indicates it was at this location after 1966.

The cockpit canopy is ajar on F-104A-20-LO 56-0791, assigned to the 83rd Fighter-Interceptor Squadron, at Taoyuan Air Base in Taiwan, on September 15, 1958. In the background, another F-104A Starfighter is parked in a revetment. The Quemoy-Matsu Crisis occurred in September 1958, over territorial rights in the Taiwan Strait. When a dispute between the People's Republic of China and the Republic of China (Taiwan) threatened to expand into full-scale war, elements of the US Air Force were sent to Taiwan to bolster that island country's armed forces.

F-104A-20-LO 56-0791, with a gray-over-white camouflage scheme, is displayed at Peterson Field in Colorado Springs, Colorado, as part of a North American Air Defense Command (NORAD) weapons display on May 24, 1965. The placard in front of the nose gear cites the plane's approximate cost at $1,763,000. *National Archives*

F-104A-20-LO 56-0844, of the 331st Fighter-Interceptor Squadron, prepares for a mission at Webb Air Force Base in Big Spring, Texas, on November 30, 1965. The enclosure over the electronics bay is open, aft of the cockpit, with some of the self-contained avionics packages visible.

Three F-104As fly in formation over Miami Beach, Florida, with the Fontainbleau Hotel at the center. The second plane, F-104A-20-LO 56-0810, served with several different squadrons and was with the 319th Fighter-Interceptor Squadron when it crashed in Florida in 1966.

A protective cover is secured to the cockpit canopy of F-104-15-LO, USAF serial number 56-0767, at McClellan Air Force Base in California on October 28, 1967. The plane is loaded with 170-gallon drop tanks on the wingtips as well as the underwing pylons. Next in line is F-104B-5-LO 57-1296, with that model's extended vertical tail.

F-104A-25-LO, USAF serial number 56-0827, *foreground*, and F-104A-15-LO 56-0782 fly in tight formation. Each plane is armed with Sidewinder missiles on wingtip rail launchers. They are painted light gray, with bare-metal areas toward the rear of the fuselage.

F-104A-20-LO, USAF serial number 56-0791, is sealed and covered for long-term storage in the dry desert air at Davis-Monthan Air Force Base in Arizona on January 9, 1969. This plane previously had served with the 4667th Combat Crew Training Squadron.

A group of F-104A Starfighters remain in long-term storage at Davis-Monthan Air Force Base in Arizona on January 9, 1969. Sealant and covers have been applied to help preserve the planes. The nearest aircraft is F-104A-20-LO 56-0811. The dry desert environment, high altitude, and alkaline soil reduce corrosion and rust on stored aircraft.

Lockheed F-104A-20-LO, serial number 56-0790, is on static display near the West Gate of Edwards Air Force Base. This plane was delivered to the US Air Force in 1957. Two years later, Lockheed leased the plane and modernized it to F-104G standards, for use in systems tests and the testing of nuclear-weapon shapes. From 1966 to the late 1970s, NASA operated this aircraft at Dryden Flight Research Center, at Edwards Air Force Base, designating it NASA 820. *David Dwight Jackson*

Lockheed F-104A-20-LO, serial number 56-0817, was photographed while it was on display at Warner Robins Air Force Base, Georgia. This Starfighter is now at the Pacific Aviation Museum, Honolulu, Hawaii. The left sides of the windscreen and cockpit canopy are shown, with a pilot's helmet hanging from the headrest. Below the canopy is the nomenclature and serial number stencil. *Author*

The right side of the fuselage of F-104A-20-LO, serial number 56-0817, below the cockpit canopy, is depicted. The yellow shape above the letter "C" is the external canopy-release handle. *Author*

On the left wingtip is the Sidewinder missile launcher rail. Also in view are the left leading-edge flap and the wing fillet. Foam blocks have been placed on the front and rear of the rail to protect viewers from injury. *Author*

The rear part of the left missile launcher rail is in the foreground, with a foam block on the rear of it. "NO STEP" stickers are on the left aileron and the left flap. *Author*

The left side of the tail fin and rudder of F-104A-20-LO, serial number 56-0817, are displayed, as well as the left side of the one-piece, all-moving tailplane. The insignia of the 83rd Fighter-Interceptor Squadron, featuring a horseshoe, ace of spades, and thunderbolt, is on the tail. *Author*

The empennage of the third F-104A-1-LO, serial number 56-0732, is observed from the left side, with the insignia of the 319th Fighter Squadron on the tail fin. The photo was taken while the plane was displayed at the Octave Chanute Museum (since closed), in Rantoul, Illinois. The Starfighter is now displayed at the Air Park at McGhee Tyson Air National Guard Base, Knoxville, Tennessee. This plane was built as a nonflying airframe, used for testing purposes. *Author*

The riveted construction of the curved fairing above the variable-area afterburner nozzle of F-104A-20-LO, serial number 56-0817, is seen from below. Above it is the trailing edge of the rudder. *Author*

While displayed at Warner Robins Air Force Base, the right wing of F-104A-20-LO, serial number 56-0817, was detached and stored upright above the wing root, as seen from the rear. Below the wing root are the right main landing gear and the bay door. *Author*

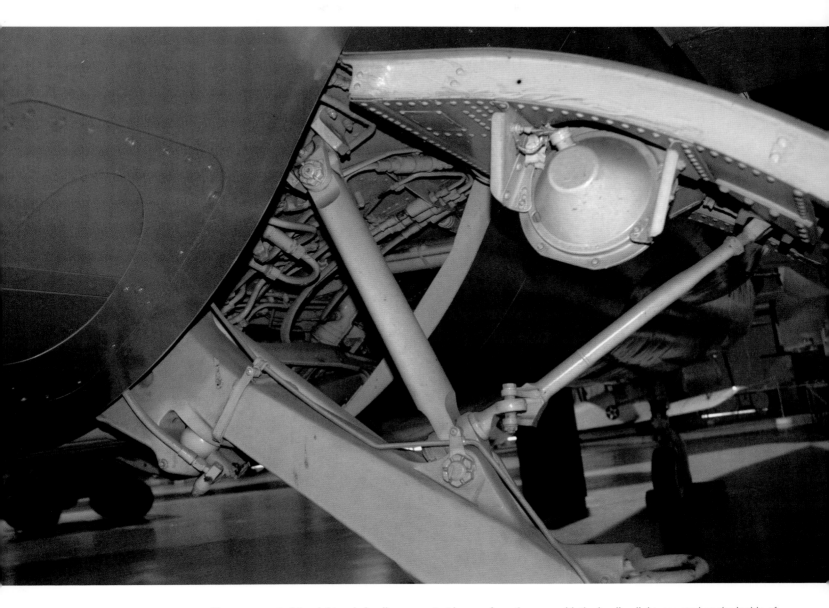

The upper part of the right main landing-gear strut is seen from the rear, with the landing light mounted on the inside of the gear bay door toward the top. The nose landing gear is visible in the background. *Author*

The right wheel, tire, and strut are observed from the rear. The main landing gear retracted forward into the bays by hydraulic power. Each main-gear wheel had hydraulic antiskid brakes. *Author*

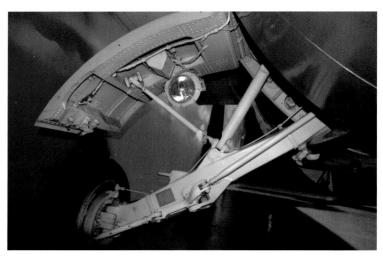

The right main landing gear is seen from the front, showing the strut, links, bay door, wheel, tire, and landing light. *Author*

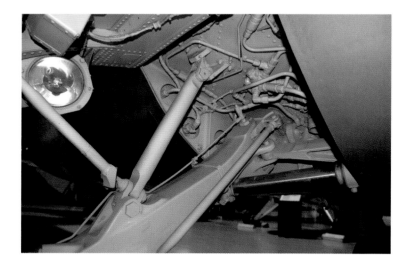

The rear of the right main landing-gear bay is visible, with plumbing, the landing light, and the door-retraction link (*left*) in evidence. The original shock absorber was replaced by a simple metal support (*center*), evidently to immobilize the landing gear during its long period on static display. The dark tube along the bottom of the landing-gear bay is the retraction piston. *Author*

In a view of the main landing-gear bays facing forward, to the sides are the landing-gear retraction cylinders and pistons. The forward bay doors are ajar. *Author*

To the rear of the port for the M61 Vulcan cannon on the left side of the forward fuselage of F-104A-1-LO, serial number 56-0732, is a swelling, to provide clearance for the six rotating barrels of the gun. To the right is the removable forward fairing of the M61 bay. *Author*

As seen in a frontal photo of the nose landing gear of F-104A-20-LO, serial number 56-0817, the wheel was mounted on an oleo strut. The gear was steerable and retracted forward into its bay. *Author*

The same nose landing gear is seen from the right side. The antitorque "scissors" link has been disconnected. *Author*

In the nose landing-gear bay, facing aft, are the operating mechanisms for the doors and strut, as well as a landing light and, at the center, the lock for the nose gear when retracted. Below and to the left of the landing light is a shackle, for towing or tying down the aircraft. *Author*

NF-104A 56-0760, one of the three aerospace trainer NF-104 models, speeds through the air with the assist of a rocket engine. F-104As with USAF serial numbers 56-0756, 56-0760, and 56-0762 were modified by Lockheed for use as aerospace trainers for the US Air Force. This training familiarized pilots with aspects of space flight, such as boost, suborbital operation, zero-gravity operation, and reentry maneuvering. At the rear of the plane was a 6,000-pound-thrust rocket engine. The NF-104A also featured extended wingtips and reaction controls—small rockets to maneuver the plane in the thin air at high altitudes. *National Archives*

The second NF-104A, 56-0760, is manned on a runway at Edwards Air Force Base in California in September 1964. The left reaction controls are on the dark, rectangular panel on the side of the nose. Other reaction controls were located on the wingtips of the NF-104A. *National Archives*

One of the NF-104As is parked at Edwards Air Force Base in September 1964. There were reaction controls with two jet motors each on both sides of the nose for yaw control, as well as on the top and the bottom of the nose for pitch control. The wingtip jets controlled roll. *National Archives*

Lockheed NF-104A 56-0760 is parked on a lake bed at Edwards Air Force Base on February 4, 1965. The engine shock cones of the NF-104As were redesigned from the F-104A versions to better handle the higher Mach numbers the NF-104A was able to reach. *National Archives*

NF-104A 56-0760 is parked at Edwards Air Force Base in September 1964. Famed test pilot Chuck Yeager flew one of the NF-104As on December 10, 1963, when the plane went into an uncontrollable spin at 101,000 feet. Yeager bailed out before the plane crashed. *National Archives*

Each NF-104A had a Rocketdyne AR2-3 rocket engine in the tail. The liquid rocket engine took over in the thin air of very high altitudes, where the plane's jet engine, which depended on oxygen for combustion, could not operate effectively. The rocket engine was mounted at an upward angle. It used JP-4 fuel along with hydrogen peroxide and had a thrust of 6,000 pounds.

In addition to thrust given to the NF-104A at high altitudes, the Rocketdyne AR2-3 engine also allowed the plane to reach altitudes of more than 118,000 feet. A zoom climb maneuver was executed through a 3.5 g pull-up at Mach 2.15 that begins at approximately 35,000 feet. The J79 engine was shut down at approximately 75,000 feet, while the AR2-3 engine took over to almost the top of the climb.

The reaction controls on the top of the nose are visible as a light-colored rectangle with two holes on it on this NF-104A aerospace trainer. The top reaction controls, when operated, forced the nose downward, while the bottom reaction controls had the opposite effect. The NF-104A's reaction controls were similar to the ones used on spacecraft to regulate roll, pitch, and yaw. *National Archives*

An NF-104A fires its rocket engine during a high-altitude zoom-climb maneuver. The NF-104A remained in service until the end of 1971, when the two remaining NF-104As were retired. Upon retirement, the NF-104As had served as a trainer aircraft for about fifty students of the Aerospace Research Pilots School, who completed a total of 301 flights in these rocket-powered Starfighters. *National Archives*

Mounted on a pylon, with landing gear retracted, NF-104A serial number 56-0760 is on static display at the Air Force Test Pilot School, Edwards Air Force Base, California. Jutting from the rear of the aircraft, below the rudder, is the pod for the 6,000-pound-thrust rocket engine. The shock cones in the engine intakes were of a different design than those on stock F-104s.

In 1959 and 1960, Lockheed Aircraft and Sperry-Phoenix converted twenty-four YF-104As and F-104As to QF-104A high-speed target drones. Their external appearance was similar to the F-104A. The difference was that the QF-104As were equipped to be flown by remote control, using radio signals. The plane also was equipped with a fully functional cockpit that allowed a pilot to fly the plane on test flights and ferry flights. This example, 55-2957, was based on the third YF-104A and was painted orange with white wings, for high visibility. QF-104 drones could be remotely flown from either the ground or air.

F-104A 56-0739 was converted to a QF-104A (sometimes known as JQF-104A—the J designated a reversible modification) configuration in April 1960. Like other QF-104s, it was assigned to the 3205th Drone Squadron. It was shot down by a GAR-2B (Falcon) missile on October 8, 1963. *San Diego Air & Space Museum*

JQF-104A 56-0735, a modified QF-104A converted from the sixth F-104A-1-LO, is maintained at Eglin Air Force Base in 1967. The buzz number on the fuselage is QFG-735. The insignia of US Air Force Systems Command is on the fuselage above the shock cone.

JQF-104A-1-LO, USAF serial number 56-0735, undergoes maintenance on a hardstand at Eglin Air Force Base in September 1964. This drone served with the 3205th Drone Squadron. The buzz number on the rear of the fuselage was QFG-735.

Lockheed/Sperry-Phoenix QF-104A-5-LO 56-0741 is parked at Eglin Air Force Base in Florida in 1971. The 3205th Drone Squadron operated all of the operational QF-104As. These drones remained in service with the US Air Force until the early 1970s.

F-104 DEVELOPMENT

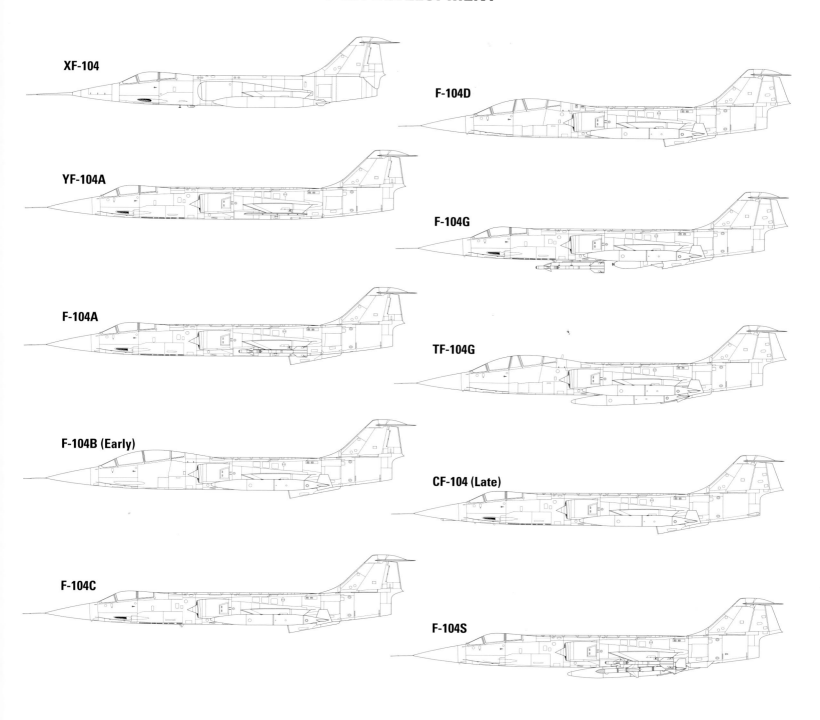

XF-104

YF-104A

F-104A

F-104B (Early)

F-104C

F-104D

F-104G

TF-104G

CF-104 (Late)

F-104S

CHAPTER 4
The Two-Seater Starfighter: F-104B

The second version of the Starfighter to enter series production was the F-104B. It was a two-seat version intended primarily as a training aircraft. Ideally, the F-104B would have the same performance and combat capability as the F-104A. However, reality dictated differently. To make room for the second seat, the 20 mm cannon was deleted. The relocation of some avionics was also required. Internal fuel capacity was reduced from 897 gallons to 752 gallons, and range decreased accordingly. The addition of the second seat also required a change in the front landing gear, which retracted to the rear on the F-104B, unlike the forward-retracting gear of the F-104A.

The first F-104B, serial number 56-3719, was hand-built. It began with an F-104A airframe that included the standard F-104A tail but lacked the ventral fin installed on the F-104A. The first F-104B flight took place on January 16, 1957. It was found that the aircraft had a tendency to snake across the sky in subsequent tests. To correct this, the ventral fin of an F-104A was installed and—more significantly—a much-larger vertical fin and broad-chord, power-assisted rudder were installed. These changes—evidenced by the rudder, which extended well past the end of the engine exhaust—remedied the problem. The changes were incorporated in the twenty-five F-104Bs assembled on production lines as well as models F-104D and beyond.

The 83rd Fighter-Interceptor Squadron, at Hamilton AFB in California, was the first operational unit to receive the F-104B. Ultimately, all three of the Air Defense Command Starfighter squadrons were issued four trainer aircraft per squadron. The final F-104B was delivered in November 1958. By 1960 the USAF began to transfer examples to allied nations. Those nations included Pakistan, the Republic of China, and the Royal Jordanian Air Force.

Pilots prepare for a training flight in "Double Trouble" at McGhee Tyson Airport in Knoxville, Tennessee, in June 1960. Lockheed produced and delivered twenty-six F-104Bs, a two-seat trainer version of the F-104A. It featured dual flight controls and instruments as well as an enlarged canopy with two hatches hinged on their left sides. The F-104B maintained the same overall dimensions as the F-104A. Components were rearranged or eliminated to make space for an extra seat to the rear of the original cockpit.

F-104B-1-LO, USAF serial number 56-3719, was the first of the F-104B series. The F-104B was powered by the same J79-GE-3A (and later, J79-GE-3B) turbojet engine as the F-104A. This plane exhibits the vertical tail as originally installed on the F-104Bs, which was identical to the F-104As. It is distinguished by the trailing edge of the rudder, which is in line with the rear of the engine nozzle. The plane exhibited a tendency to weave during tests. Subsequently, an enlarged vertical tail and a ventral fin were introduced to solve the problem. *National Archives*

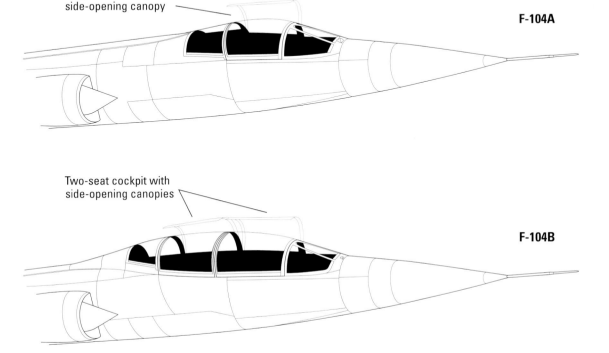

Single-seat cockpit with side-opening canopy

F-104A

Two-seat cockpit with side-opening canopies

F-104B

The differences between the F-104A and F-104B canopies are illustrated. The F-104A featured a canopy that was hinged on the left side. The F-104B had two canopies, one for each crewman. These canopies were hinged on the left and did not have any structure to separate them.

F-104B-1-LO, USAF serial number 56-3722, parks at Edwards Air Force Base on April 16, 1959. It was the fourth trainer. Initially, the F-104Bs lacked a ventral fin, but most F-104Bs were retrofitted with these fins as well as extended vertical tails to solve stability problems. The enlarged vertical tail extended significantly to the rear of the exhaust nozzle. The front and rear canopies shared a joint between them. This feature would change in subsequent models of two-seat Starfighters. *National Archives*

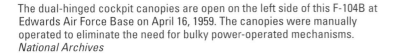

The dual-hinged cockpit canopies are open on the left side of this F-104B at Edwards Air Force Base on April 16, 1959. The canopies were manually operated to eliminate the need for bulky power-operated mechanisms. *National Archives*

Lockheed F-104B-10-LO, USAF serial number 57-1304, was one of the F-104Bs that were converted to upward-firing ejector seats and retrofitted with a fixed transparent section between the front and rear jettisonable canopies.

The fourth F-104B—F-104B-1-NO, USAF serial number 56-3722—is exhibited at an open house. To the rear of the aft cockpit is an insignia. "AFSC" (Air Force Systems Command) is inscribed above it, while the lower markings are "AERONAUTICAL SYSTEMS DIVISION." The production Starfighters had an inlet within an inlet on the shock cone to introduce cooling air to the engine compartment. The inlet is visible on the part of the shock cone inside the inlet.

Guests inspect F-104B-1-LO, USAF serial number 56-3722, during an exhibition. The insignia of the Air Research and Development Command is on the fuselage between the Air Force Systems Command and the Aeronautical Systems Division legends. The unit was redesignated to the Air Force Systems Command in 1961. Below the tail number is another insignia, which features a shield, a light-colored triangle, and two biplanes.

An air-data probe is attached to the nose of the first F-104B-1-LO, USAF serial number 56-3719, prior to a flight test of the aircraft. The nose landing gear was moved to the front end of the gear bay on the F-104B. The landing gear consequently swiveled to the rear during retraction.

F-104B-1-LO 56-2719 features a retrofitted vertical tail and ventral fin at the Air Force Flight Testing Center on Edwards Air Force Base on January 31, 1958. The enlarged tail is identifiable because it juts to the rear of the jet nozzle. *National Archives*

An F-104B is chocked at the Air Force Flight Test Center at Edwards Air Force Base, California, on January 31, 1958. From the front, the F-104B looked similar to the F-104A except for the enlarged cockpit canopy. *National Archives*

F-104B-1-LO, USAF serial number 56-3719, features two short antennas on the underside of the forward part of the fuselage. A thickened area is located at the upper end of each of the antennas. A small letter *B* is marked on the nose.

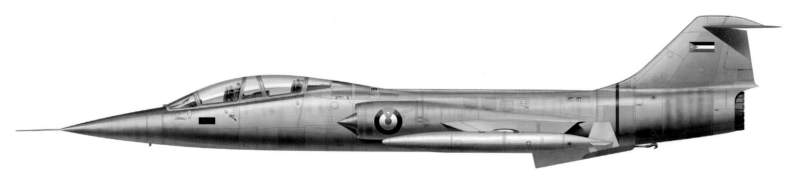

Three F-104Bs served with No. 9 Squadron, Royal Jordanian Air Force, as conversion trainers. Each trainer bore the flag of Jordan on the vertical tail and the Royal Jordanian Air Force roundel on the wings and inlets. The roundel consists of black, white, and green circles with a wedge-shaped overlay at the top with a white star. The United States supplied thirty-six early-type Starfighters to Silâḥ al-Jaw al-Malakiyah al-Urduniyah, or the Royal Jordanian Air Force, in spring 1967. Four more were supplied in late 1968.

Preserved at the Aerospace Museum of California, McClellan, California, since July 1983, is the third F-104B-10-LO Starfighter, serial number 57-1303. This aircraft was delivered to the US Air Force on October 2, 1958, and it served at the NASA Ames Research Center, NAS Moffett Field, California, from October 1958 to around April 1978, flying as NASA 71303 and acquiring the nickname "Howling Howland." *David Dwight Jackson*

CHAPTER 5
More Power: F-104C and D

The F-104C was developed to counter some of the criticism leveled at the F-104A. Specifically, the F-104C incorporated in-flight refueling capability to counter TAC's criticism of the F-104A's limited endurance. This in-flight refueling capability was achieved by the introduction of a fixed but removable refueling probe, which was located on the left side of the fuselage.

In an effort to improve the all-weather capabilities of the Starfighter, the F-104C had an improved fire-control radar, the AN/ASG-14T-2. This allowed the aircraft to function as a night fighter, although it did not have all-weather capability. TAC's concern about the modest offensive capability of the Starfighter was also addressed, this in an extreme manner, by adding five stores pylons: one on the aircraft centerline and two under each wing. The centerline pylon, which had a 2,000-pound capacity, could accommodate one Mk. 28 or Mk. 43 nuclear weapon. This arsenal joined the internal M61A1 20 mm Vulcan Gatling gun.

The F-104C was powered by a J79-GE-7, as opposed to the J79-GE-3 found in the F-104A. The J79-GE-7 generated substantially more power, producing 10,000 pounds of static thrust and 15,800 pounds with afterburner.

A contract calling for the production of fifty-six examples of the F-104C was signed on March 2, 1956. This was followed on December 26, 1956, with an order for twenty-one more aircraft. Later, a further 363 F-104Cs were ordered, although ultimately those were canceled, thereby limiting F-104C production to the first seventy-seven examples contracted. The first flight of the F-104C occurred on July 24, 1958.

While the J79-GE-7 engine, which was 3 inches larger in diameter than the J79-GE-3, did prove more powerful, power-plant-related issues continued to plague the Starfighter. By 1963, forty serious incidents had occurred with the aircraft, resulting in the loss of twenty-four Starfighters and killing nine pilots. Project Seven Up was launched by General Electric in May 1963. Running through June 1964, the project introduced a number of modifications to the engine.

On December 14, 1959, even before the engine problems had been corrected, USAF captain "Joe" B. Jordan took off from Edwards Air Force Base flying F-104C 56–0885. He climbed to an altitude of 103,389 feet, setting a world altitude record. In the process the F-104C became the first aircraft to take off under its own power and climb to over 100,000 feet.

Just as the F-104B was a two-seat combat trainer version of the F-104A, the F-104D was the two-seat trainer equivalent of the F-104C. As with the F-104B, the F-104D featured a longer canopy, a rearward-retracting nose landing gear, and a larger tail than its single-seat counterpart. The two-seat models also lacked the 20 mm automatic cannon and had reduced fuel capacity, yielding shorter range. Twenty-one examples were built, the first of which flew on October 31, 1958.

The Lockheed F-104C was an effort to field a tactical fighter-bomber/interceptor version of the Starfighter to replace the North American F-100 Super Sabre. It was similar in design to the F-104A, but it featured a much more powerful J79-GE-7A engine, a fixed—but removable—refueling probe, provisions for additional bomb pylons, and under-fuselage pylons for eventual AIM-9 Sidewinder missiles. Lockheed produced a total of seventy-seven F-104Cs.

The first of the F-104Cs, 56-0833, takes off from Lockheed's Palmdale, California, plant en route to Nellis Air Force Base in Nevada. It joined the Tactical Air Command before it was assigned to the 831st Air Division at George Air Force Base in California. *National Archives*

Model	XF-104	F-104A	F-104B	F-104C	F-104G	F-104S
Crew	1	1	2	1	1	1
Power plant	J65-B-3	J79-GE-3	J79-GE-3	J79-GE-7A	J79-GE-11A	J79-GE-19
Wingspan	21' 11"	21' 9"	21' 9"	21' 9"	21' 9"	21' 9"
Length	49' 2"	54' 8"	54' 8"	54' 8"	54' 8"	54' 9"
Height	13' 6"	13' 5"	13' 5"	13' 5"	13' 5"	13' 6"
Wing area (ft.²)	196.1	196.1	196.1	196.1	196.1	196.1
Empty weight (lbs.)	15,000	13,384	13,327	12,760	13,966	14,900
Max. weight (lbs.)	15,700	25,840	24,912	27,853	29,038	31,000
Combat weight	NA	17,988	17,812	19,470	20,640	21,690
Max. speed (mph) @ altitude in ft.	1,324 @ 50,000	1,037 @ 50,000	1,145 @ 65,000	1,150 @ 50,000	1,146 @ 50,000	1,450 @ 36,000
Cruise speed (mph)	n/a	519	516	510	510	610
Max. rate of climb (ft. min.)	n/a	60,395	64,500	54,000	48,000	55,000
Service ceiling (ft.)	50,500	64,975	64,975	58,000	50,000	58,000
Normal range (miles)	800	730	460	850	1,080	1,550
Maximum range (miles)	n/a	1,400	1,225	1,500	1,630	1,815
Flyaway cost (millions*)	n/a	$1.7	$2.4	$1.5	$1.42	n/a
Maintenance cost per flying hour*	n/a	$395	$544	$395	n/a	n/a

* 1960 dollars

Lockheed F-104C-5-LO 56-0833 executes a climb during an early flight in 1958. The refueling probe was not installed. The elongated port for the M61 20 mm cannon is visible below the letters "US" in the "US AIR FORCE" marking.

F-104C-5-LO 56-0833 was almost visually identical to the F-104A. The F-104C's first production block was numbered 5 instead of the traditional 1; hence, F-104C-5-LO from block 1.

Lockheed F-104C-5-LO, USAF serial number 56-0833, flies overhead during its flight from Lockheed's Palmdale plant to Nellis Air Force Base. The refueling probe was not installed but was important for the long-distance deployments that were planned for the F-104C. *National Archives*

An F-104C receives fuel from a tanker during a long-distance flight. First, the pilot of the Starfighter coordinated his speed and course with those of the tanker. Then, he carefully maneuvered his plane up to the refueling drogue of the tanker to refuel.

Four F-104Cs fly in close formation. All four planes are F-104C-10-LOs—as determined by their tail numbers. For example, 70926 translates to USAF serial number 57-0926. All four planes have the insignia of Tactical Air Command on their vertical tails.

F-104Cs are parked on a tarmac at Myrtle Beach Air Force Base in South Carolina during Swift Strike III, joint USAF-Army maneuvers held in the Carolinas during July and August 1963. The second plane is F-104C-5-LO, USAF serial number 56-0922.

Ordnance and stores are displayed in front of an F-104C assigned to the 479th Tactical Fighter Wing at George Air Force Base in California. These include two AIM-9B Sidewinder missiles, an M61 20 mm cannon, a LAU-3A rocket-launcher pod, a Mk. 28 nuclear weapon shape (the "special weapon practice unit").

F-104C, USAF serial number 56-0929, of the 436th Tactical Fighter Squadron (TFS), is towed from an open-ended alert hangar before its departure for the States in 1964. The refueling probe is black with a yellow elbow and fairing. Starfighters of the 436th TFS of the 479th Tactical Fighter Wing deployed to Morón Air Base in Spain to provide defense for Strategic Air Command B-47 bombers based there in August 1960. The 436th TFS remained at Morón until 1963, when it was replaced by the 334th TFS.

Crews prepare several rows of Starfighters along a hardstand at an unidentified Air Force base. Bombs are ready and lined up for quick attachment. The aircraft to the left is USAF serial number 57-0923, an F-104C-10-LO. Buzz number FG-923 is marked on its fuselage. The F-104 on the right has white and red bands on its pitot-tube mast. In the center background is an F-105 Thunderchief.

F-104C-10-LO 57-0925 taxis prior to takeoff during Exercise Coulee Crest, a joint Army–Air Force maneuver, at Fairchild Air Force Base in Washington in 1963. The Starfighter with red bands on the fuselage is assigned to the "Red" Air Force in this exercise.

F-104Cs of the 435th Tactical Fighter Squadron, based at George Air Force Base in California, line up at Fairchild Air Force Base in the spring of 1963 for Exercise Coulee Crest. The fourth plane from the left is F-104C-10-LO 57-0925.

F-104C-5-LO, USAF serial number 56-0903, is parked at Tân Sơn Nhứt Air Base in the Republic of Vietnam in 1965. The antiglare panel to the canopy's front and sides is a grayish color. The radome is a lighter-gray color. Gunpowder smudges are present around the firing port for the M61 20 mm Vulcan cannon. The refueling probe and its fairing are clearly visible to the side of the cockpit. The left air brake is in the open position toward the rear of the fuselage. Another F-104C-5-LO is located to the left of the main Starfighter.

Two F-104Cs take off on a mission from Đà Nẵng, Republic of Vietnam, in December 1965. The forward ends of the refueling probes of both F-104Cs are visible to the fronts of the windscreens. Both planes carry underwing drop tanks with Sidewinder air-to-air infrared-guided missiles on the wingtips. The nearest plane is F-104C-5-LO 56-0928. On August 1, 1966, an enemy surface-to-air missile (SAM) destroyed this plane and killed the pilot, Capt. John Kwortnik of the 435th Tactical Fighter Squadron.

F-104C-5-LO 56-0892 rests on a hardstand at Tân Sơn Nhứt between missions in 1965. A 750-pound bomb is shackled to the pylon under each wing. The Tactical Air Command insignia is superimposed over a yellow lightning bolt edged in red on the vertical tail.

Aircraft lined up at Tân Sơn Nhứt Air Base in 1965 include at least six F-104Cs running from the foreground to the left background. The planes with the tail numbers that start with "6" are F-104C-5-LOs, while those with tail numbers that begin with "7" are F-104C-10-LOs.

The same flight line of F-104Cs features four Starfighters. The planes are parked within sandbag revetments. The revetments are designed to limit damage to the aircraft and prevent the spread of explosions should the area come under artillery or rocket attack.

F-104Cs of the 436th TFS at Tân Sơn Nhứt Air Base in 1965 include the same planes in the same order. The covers for the electronics bays are open on the first two Starfighters.

A pair of F-104C Starfighters fly high above the clouds. The lead plane is an F-104C-5-LO, while the other aircraft is an F-104C-10-LO. Both planes have Tactical Air Command insignia with thunderbolts on the vertical tails. The fairings of their refueling probes are painted black. The wing tops are white, and the vertical tails and the radomes are a grayish shade. Both Starfighters carry centerline drop tanks and AIM-9 Sidewinder air-to-air missiles on the wingtip launcher rails.

Three F-104Cs park behind a revetment at Tân Sơn Nhứt Air Base in the Republic of Vietnam in 1965. The closest Starfighter is F-104C-10-LO 57-0923, in the middle is F-104C-5-LO 56-0892, and F-104C-10-LO 57-0930—the final F-104C produced—is at the rear.

Two F-104C-5-LOs park next to a revetment at a base in Southeast Asia in 1965. They are USAF serial numbers 56-0902 (*in the foreground*) and 56-0886 (*in the background*). Both planes have Tactical Air Command insignia with thunderbolts on the vertical tails. The fairing for the refueling probe is painted black on the closest Starfighter. The tip of the wingtip tank is yellow. This plane was destroyed on April 23, 1968, when it went out of control during a high-altitude, high-speed flight control test.

Three F-104Cs are parked in a single revetment at Tân Sơn Nhứt Air Base in the Republic of Vietnam in 1965. The Starfighters are, *from left to right*, F-104C-10-LO 57-0921, F-104C-10-LO 57-0927, and F-104C-5-LO, tail number 56-0903. The revetments are more sophisticated than the average sandbag variety. These revetments feature perforated steel barriers to the rear and concrete barriers to the sides. The pitot-tube masts are decorated with red and white bands.

Two F-104Cs speed along on a mission to bomb an enemy target in Vietnam in November 1966. They are painted in an early version of the Southeast Asia camouflage. It is a mix of greens, tan, and gray. Each plane carries two 750-pound bombs on wing pylons.

Crews work around F-104 Starfighters deployed to Udorn Royal Thai Air Base in Thailand in 1968. The planes are painted in Southeast Asia camouflage, which includes tan and two shades of green over light gray. All Starfighters have refueling probes installed. The second and third planes are, respectively, F-104C-10-LO 57-0928, and F-104C-10-LO 57-0927. To the far right is another line of F-104s. They also bear the Southeast Asia camouflage.

An F-104C in Southeast Asia camouflage connects to the drogue of a KC-135 tanker during a refueling operation over the Pacific in October 1966. *National Archives*

Two F-104Cs fly off the right wing of a KC-135 tanker after they refueled over the Pacific Ocean, in October 1966. The nearest Starfighter is F-104C-10-LO, USAF serial number 57-0928. Each plane has two horizontal yellow bars on the lower part of the rudder. *National Archives*

A crew maintains and prepares an F-104C painted in Southeast Asia camouflage for a mission. A fitted cover is installed on the inlet to prevent the introduction of foreign objects that could damage or destroy the engine.

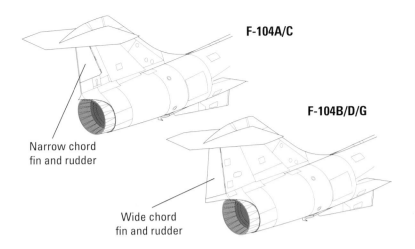

F-104A/C

F-104B/D/G

Narrow chord
fin and rudder

Wide chord
fin and rudder

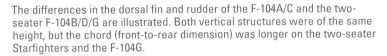

The differences in the dorsal fin and rudder of the F-104A/C and the two-seater F-104B/D/G are illustrated. Both vertical structures were of the same height, but the chord (front-to-rear dimension) was longer on the two-seater Starfighters and the F-104G.

Lockheed F-104C-5-LO, serial number 56-0914, is preserved at the National Museum of the US Air Force, at Wright-Patterson Air Force Base, Ohio. It sports the fixed refueling probe that was a key distinguishing feature of this model of Starfighter. Buzz number FG-914 is marked on the aft part of the fuselage.

Auxiliary fuel tanks are on the wingtips of F-104C-5-LO, serial number 56-0914. The fairing for the M61 Vulcan cannon is evident below the "US AIR FORCE" marking on the forward fuselage. Red and white "candy stripes" are on the pitot / static probe on the nose.

Using a tow bar, a tractor is positioning the F-104C on the floor of the National Museum of the US Air Force. It will rest under the right wing of a Martin EB-57D Canberra electronic-countermeasures aircraft.

Details of the refueling probe of the F-104C at the National Museum of the US Air Force are displayed. Also in view are the nomenclature and serial-number stencil and the door, outlined in yellow, for the external control for jettisoning the canopy. *Author*

The base of the refueling probe is shown close-up. Above the letter "I" in "AIR" is an angle-of-attack sensor. *Author*

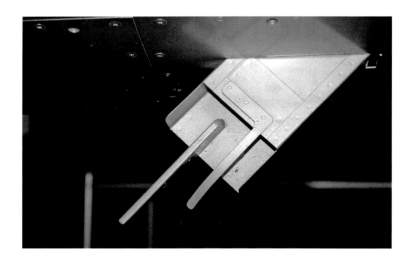

On the bottom of the fuselage, aft of the nose landing-gear bay, is this link ejector chute, for the M61 Vulcan cannon. *Author*

The right engine intake and shock cone of the F-104C at the National Museum of the US Air Force are in view. The shock cone, also known as the conical ramp, served to optimize the ram effect during operations above Mach 1.5.

A viewing platform is set up on the right side of the F-104C. The yellow object to the rear of the right wing is an MA-1A start cart, which generated high-velocity air for spooling up the jet engine to sufficient rpm for it to start.

The cockpit of the F-104C at the National Museum of the US Air Force is viewed from above the pan of the ejection seat. To the front of the seat pan is the yellow-and-black ejection handle. The yellow-and-black D ring to the side of the control stick is the canopy-release handle. On the instrument panel to the front of the grip of the control stick is the radarscope. To the left is the light-colored engine throttle control.

A wide-angle view of the F-104C cockpit canopy and interior is available from the platform along the right side of the forward fuselage. Above the ejection seat, manufactured by Stanley Aviation Corporation, is the red headrest. The yellow-and-black oblong ring to the rear of the headrest is for manually cutting the cables that automatically pulled the pilot's feet back to the base of the seat pan just prior to ejection.

F-104D-15-LO 57-1334 is the last of the F-104Ds. Similar in concept to the F-104B, the Lockheed F-104D was a two-seat combat trainer. However, it was based on the F-104C, whereas the F-104B was based on the F-104A. The F-104D was powered by the General Electric J79-GE-7 engine, and it included the enlarged vertical tail and the ventral fin used on the F-104B for enhanced stability. Lockheed completed a total of twenty-one F-104Ds, with deliveries occurring between November 1958 and August 1959. The Air Force assigned all F-104Ds to the 479th Tactical Fighter Wing. Shortly after these planes were delivered, the ejector seats were converted from downward ejecting to upward ejecting, which necessitated a total redesign of the canopy. The new canopy included an additional fixed section between the front and rear side-opening sections.

A crew prepares F-104D-15-LO 57-13333 for flight at George Air Force Base in California in 1963. In continuance of the original F-104C design, the Lockheed F-104D featured a nonretractable—but removable—refueling probe on the left side of the fuselage.

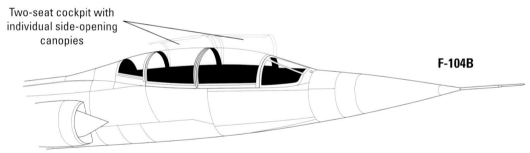

Two-seat cockpit with individual side-opening canopies

F-104B

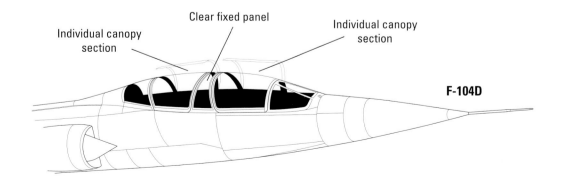

Individual canopy section

Clear fixed panel

Individual canopy section

F-104D

The upper diagram shows the F-104B canopy with two left-hinged panels. They share a common joint when closed. The lower diagram shows the F-104D canopy as modified for upward-ejecting seats, with a fixed, clear section between the two crew-access sections.

F-104D-10-LO 57-1323, the third of the series, is displayed at Eglin Air Force Base in Florida, in 1971, without a refueling probe. Although the upward-firing ejection seats necessitated a drastic redesign of the cockpit canopy, the canopy's crew-access panels remained hinged on the left side.

CHAPTER 6
The Starfighter for Everyone: F-104G

One of the largest operators of the F-104 was the Federal Republic of Germany (West Germany). The F-104 was selected on November 6, 1958, after a fly-off competition with the Grumman F11F-1F Super Tiger.

The Starfighter variant selected for the Luftwaffe, and later for the Bundesmarine, was the F-104G. The F-104G utilized the larger tail with a fully powered rudder as found on the F-104B and D. It also featured a strengthened airframe, enlarged main landing gear, enlarged tires, and leading-edge full-span flaps for combat maneuvers. As initially delivered, the F-104G used the Lockheed C-2 upward-firing ejection seat, while the USAF still used the downward-firing seat. Later, the Luftwaffe replaced the C-2 ejection seat with the Martin-Baker GQ-7 (F) zero-zero upward-firing seat.

A formal contract was signed on March 18, 1959, for the production of these aircraft in Europe under license. The Luftwaffe and other NATO allies signed similar contracts. Lockheed built 139 F-104Gs in California. The initial example first flew on June 7, 1960. The Lockheed-built aircraft were supplied to Germany, Greece, Norway, and Turkey. Pattern aircraft were also delivered to manufacturers in Belgium and Italy.

European production was distributed among four groups, on the basis of geographical location. The South Group included Dornier at Munich, Heinkel at Speyer, Messerschmitt at Augsburg, and Siebel at Donauworth. BMW at Koblenz was licensed for J79 production. The North Group comprised Fokker at Schipol and Dordrech and Aviolanda at Papendrecht, plus Focke-Wulf at Bremen, Hamburger Flugzeugbau in Hamburg, and Weserflugzeugbau at Einswarden. The West Group consisted of SABCA (Société Anonyme Belge de Constructions Aéronautiques) and Fairey S.A. of Belgium. J79 production for this group was by Fabrique Nationale in Brussels. An Italian Group was formed by Fiat at Turin, with Aerfer-Macchi, Piaggio, SACA, and SIAI-Marchetti serving as subcontractors. F-104Gs built by the various manufacturers totaled 1,122.

Germany's first Lockheed-produced F-104G flies in November 1960. The F-104G was an all-weather, multirole strike-fighter that was the most numerous version of the Starfighter. It was a strengthened version of the F-104C. It also featured a larger vertical tail and improved avionics. Lockheed initially produced this version and provided additional examples as necessary. However, the F-104G and its components also were produced by a number of companies. Alternative manufacturers included SABCA/Fairey in Belgium; Canadair in Canada; Dornier, Focke Wulf, and Messerschmitt in Germany; Fiat in Italy; Mitsubishi in Japan; and Fokker in the Netherlands. A total of 1,127 F-104Gs were produced. *National Archives*

This F-104G was operated by Erprobungsstelle 61 (ErpSt 61), or Luftwaffe Test Unit 61, from Manching Air Base. It is shown with a Nord AS-30 air-to-surface missile under the left wing. The aircraft was assembled by Messerschmitt at Manching utilizing parts from Lockheed. Assembly began on November 28, 1961, and the aircraft was accepted by the Luftwaffe on June 8, 1962. The aircraft was relegated for use as a static trainer on April 11, 1984, and survives today as a monument at Lechfeld Air Base. *Hans-Heiri Stapfer*

Representative F-104Gs of three air forces fly in formation. From front to rear are the Federal Republic of Germany's Luftwaffe, which features a iron cross; the Royal Canadian Air Force (designated the CF-104), which features a blue-and-white roundel with a red maple leaf in the center; and the Japanese Air Self-Defense Force (designated the F-104J), which features the traditional Hinomaru of a red circle with a thin white border.

The German aircraft is fitted with wingtip fuel tanks to extend the range of the F-104G. The tanks are important due to limited internal fuel capacity and potentially high fuel consumption rates. A jet engine's fuel efficiency is normally defined as thrust-specific fuel consumption. It is always expressed in weight (pounds or kilograms) of fuel burned per hour divided by the thrust (pounds or newtons) generated. The weight of the fuel is used in this calculation rather than volume (gallons or liters) because volume varies with temperature, which decreases as altitude increases.

The J79-17 (similar to the J79-15 used in the F-104G), at 17,835 pounds of thrust (afterburner), burns 1.965 pounds/hour-pound of thrust. At 11,905 pounds of thrust (military power), the engine burns 0.85 pounds/hour-pound of thrust. These figures are for the engine alone, without the weight and drag of the airframe, which decrease efficiency. The F-104G has an internal fuel capacity of 852 gallons (about 5,800 pounds of fuel at sea level) and a range of 1,080 miles. Thus, at cruise speed, the Straighter burns about 1.25 gallons per mile.

As part of its role as a strike-fighter, a key feature of the F-104G was the availability of two pylons under each wing to carry bombs, auxiliary fuel tanks, and other stores. Three additional pylons were fitted to the belly of this example.

A trio of Luftwaffe F-104Gs fly in formation high above the clouds. They bear the "DA" code of the first Luftwaffe air wing to become operational with the F-104G. Jagdbombergeschwader (JBG) 31 "Boelcke" (JaBoG 31) was based at Norvenich. This wing became fully operational in late 1963.

This Luftwaffe F-104G bears the "JA" fuselage code of Jagdgeschwader 71 (JG 71) "Richthofen" as well as the number 101. Both the pilot's canopy and the section of canopy over the equipment bay to the rear of the cockpit are hinged on the left side and are open.

A German F-104G banks left during a high-altitude flight. The plane bears the "DA" code of JBG 31 and the aircraft number 109. A Sidewinder air-to-air missile is mounted on each wingtip, but the aircraft is otherwise clean of underwing and under-fuselage stores. The F-104G carried the M61 Vulcan 20 mm cannon, as well as the sophisticated North American Search and Ranging Radar (NASARR) fire-control system integrated with the bombing computer, inertial navigator, and air-data computer.

A US Air Force F-104G carries a blue-and-white practice AIM-9J Sidewinder missile on each wingtip rail during a training mission on August 1, 1979. This aircraft bore USAF serial number 63-13269, but it was built under license by Fokker in the Netherlands and had served with the Luftwaffe before being transferred to the US Air Force. The plane was assigned to the 69th Tactical Fighter Training Squadron, 58th Tactical Training Wing, Twelfth Air Force, and served as a trainer for Luftwaffe pilots at Luke Air Force Base, Arizona.

A practice bomblet falls from its dispenser on the centerline hardpoint of F-104G USAF, serial number 63-13252. Practice bomblets were a cheap and effective way to conduct bomb practice. These bomblets mimicked the ballistic properties of the authentic combat bombs.

F-104G 63-13243 rests on the tarmac at Langley Air Force Base in Virginia on March 20, 1976. The aircraft was assigned to the 58th Tactical Fighter Training Wing at Luke Air Force Base in Arizona. Bicentennial decorations are on the wingtip tank, and the wing is painted white.

Lockheed F-104G, USAF serial number 63-13249, is parked on a hardstand at McConnell Air Force Base in Kansas in September 1969. "DANGER/ARRESTING/HOOK" is stenciled on the fuselage aft of the wing. This hook was used for arrested landings on short runways.

In a view from below during flight, this F-104G, USAF serial number 63-13240, exhibits a single centerline pylon on the belly between the intakes. Though it bore USAF markings, this Starfighter was the property of the Luftwaffe and was utilized at Luke Air Force Base to train German fighter pilots.

F-104G, USAF serial number 63-13243, assigned to the 58th Tactical Fighter Wing, is parked on a hardstand around 1976. The dark-colored panel in the center of the dorsal fin was a darker panel of metal than the surrounding panels.

F-104G 63-13243 is parked on a hardstand on March 20, 1976. A commemorative United States Bicentennial decoration with the number 76 and red, white, and blue stripes is visible on the wing-tank fin.

An F-104G shows the pylon positions. Two pylons are under each wing and loaded with bombs. The centerline pylon is on the belly of the fuselage, with a bent or cranked pylon to each side of the centerline pylon.

Another F-104G with Luftwaffe markings on the wing presents a sleek, futuristic appearance. The small, dark object centered on the bottom of the windscreen frame is an infrared sensor.

A West German F-104G Starfighter and a USAF F-104A fly in formation near Edwards Air Force Base on January 9, 1962, while assigned to the F-104 Joint Test Force. While many F-104Gs were license-built by various European consortiums, both of these aircraft were built by Lockheed. The Luftwaffe aircraft, construction number 683-2059, was delivered in 1962, while the USAF Starfighter, the first of the F-104A-10-LO production block, was delivered in 1958. Despite their age and model differences, the two aircraft appear virtually identical. In July 1962, KF+134 was disassembled, airlifted to Messerschmitt-Manching, reassembled, and test-flown again on August 17, prior to assignment to a combat wing. The aircraft was lost on July 30, 1969, due to a crash on takeoff at Norvenich Air Base. Fortunately, the pilot ejected safely. F-104A 56-0748 survives today and is on display at Dyess Air Force Base in Texas. *National Archives*

A pilot stands on the hardstand near an F-104G outfitted with wingtip fuel tanks. F-104 wings were too thin to include fuel tanks. Meanwhile, the J79 engine and M61A1 gun consumed so much of the fuselage that little room remained for fuel.

Four Luftwaffe F-104Gs serving with Jagdgeschwader 74 "Mölders" fly over the Kochelsee in the Bavarian Alps in June 1965. These planes bear the typical Luftwaffe camouflage of dark green and dark gray on the upper surfaces and gray on the lower surfaces. *Bundesarchiv*

Luftwaffe F-104G DC+110 is parked on a hardstand. It was assigned to Jagdbombergeschwader 33 (abbreviated as JaBoG 33, "Fighter-Bomber Wing 33"). On the tail below the fin flash is the wing's insignia. The demarcation between the upper and lower camouflage colors is straight and quite sharp.

A Luftwaffe RF-104G with the fuselage code 24+98 is parked at RAF Woodbridge in England on August 8, 1969. This Starfighter was assigned to Aufklärungsgeschwader 52 (Reconnaissance Wing 52). The unit's insignia, which features a black panther's head and the number 52, is on the tail.

Pilots of Jagdgeschwader 74 pose in the cockpits of their F-104Gs. These Starfighters were painted in uniform camouflage patterns, but the aircraft show various degrees of weathering and freshness. The caution and informational markings are in English. The "RESCUE" sticker and canopy release instructions are yellow and black for greater visibility. Jagdgeschwader 74 flew Starfighters out of Neuberg from May 1964 to June 1974. *Bundesarchiv*

Luftwaffe F-104G JD+244 of Jagdgeschwader 74 lands with its left leading-edge flap extended. The Starfighters were equipped with leading-edge flaps to assist with low-speed maneuverability. These flaps were operated by electromechanical actuators. Additionally, bleed air from the engine was used to power boundary layer air over the trailing-edge flaps, for improved maneuverability. *Bundesarchiv*

F-104G JD+107 of Jagdgeschwader 74 deploys its drogue chute to slow to a stop. Starfighters were equipped with a drogue chute to decrease the distance from touchdown to full stop. The chute was packed into a compartment on the underside of the fuselage rear. It was of a conical-ring design with slots between the rings. The chute had a diameter of 18 feet and was manually deployed by the pilot. *Bundesarchiv*

F-104G JD+114 of Jagdgeschwader 74 "Mölders" rests on a hardstand. On the tail is the insignia of JG 74. The insignia shows a stylized delta-wing aircraft climbing above a runway. Jagdgeschwader 74 received its complement of F-104G Starfighters from 1964 to 1966. During the F-104's service with JG 74, nine planes crashed and resulted in the deaths of three pilots. A total of 298 German F-104s were lost, and 116 pilots were killed.

Mounted on the wingtip launcher rail of a German F-104G is a Sidewinder missile with safety pins and tags attached. On the wing pylon is a multiple-rocket-launcher pod. The pod fired folding-fin-stabilized air-to-ground rockets.

F-104G 23+18 of the Bundesmarine (federal German navy) is readied for a mission. It served with Marininefliegergeschwader 2 (Naval Air Wing 2), based at Eggebeck. These Starfighters were tasked with armed reconnaissance and antishipping strikes.

Luftwaffe F-104G 23+01 of Jagdbombergeschwader 34 is prepared for its next mission at Meminger Air Base in the Federal Republic of Germany in June 1971. Bilingual stencils in German and English are present. The insignia of Jagdbombergeschwader 34 is on the inlet.

Four Luftwaffe F-104Gs are being serviced outside a hangar in Manching. A portion of the variety of ground support gear needed to operate the aircraft dots the scene, not the least of which is a crew ladder for each aircraft. *Hans-Heiri Stapfer*

Personnel appear to be inspecting the connection between the wingtip fuel tank and the stub wing of this Luftwaffe F-104G. The fuel tank had a capacity of 170 gallons. *Hans-Heiri Stapfer*

RF-104G EB+126 serves with Aufklärungsgeschwader 52 (Reconnaissance Wing 52) at Leck Air Base in the Federal Republic of Germany on June 1, 1967. The RF-104G was the tactical reconnaissance version of the F-104G. It featured internal cameras and did not have an M61 cannon.

Two Luftwaffe TF-104Gs bear the "DA" fuselage codes of Jagdbombergeschwader 31 "Boelcke." To the right is DA+368 and to the left is DA+367. The TF-104G was the training version of the F-104G and equivalent to the F-104D.

US Air Force (USAF) TF-104G, serial number 61-3079, prepares to take off from an air base. The aircraft is a two-seat trainer version.

An F-104G bears the Koninklijke Luchtmacht (Royal Netherlands Air Force) insignia of a circle with red, white, and blue segments and a small orange circle in the middle. To replace its aging Republic F-84Fs and RF-84F aircraft, the Dutch air force acquired 138 total Starfighters starting in 1962. These included ninety-five F-104Gs and RF-104Gs produced by the North (Fokker) Group of the Starfighter Consortium, twenty-five F-104Gs manufactured by Fiat and the Italian Group, and eighteen Lockheed-built TF-104Gs.

A soft cover protects the inlet on a Royal Netherlands Air Force F-104G of 320 Squadron. Two Sidewinder launch rails are on the aircraft belly. The tail has the dark figures "D-8098" below a round insignia. Accidents claimed forty-three Dutch Starfighters prior to the Netherlands' November 1984 phaseout of the F-104.

Dutch F-104G D-8053 banks left over farmlands. It is painted in a monotone camouflage scheme. The 306 Squadron insignia on the tail features an eagle's head superimposed over a blue semicircle, with five white stars on the left and a light-blue semicircle on the right.

Belgian lieutenant colonel Bill Ongena executes a low-altitude roll in F-104G, serial number FX83, at an air show at Beavechain Air Base in Belgium in 1966. The Force Aérienne Belge acquired 100 F-104Gs and twelve TF-104Gs built by SABCA. They were distributed to No. 1 Wing and No. 10 Wing.

Two Belgian air force F-104Gs, serial numbers FX03 and FX04, execute a unison takeoff. The Belgian air force insignia is a roundel colored from the outside to the inside in red, yellow, and black. The lips of the inlets and the shock cones are painted a dark color.

A camouflaged Belgian air force F-104G of No. 1 Wing is parked next to a heavily weathered Starfighter at Melsbroek in Belgium on June 24, 1967. Belgium received its first F-104Gs in February 1963 and retired its last Starfighters in 1983.

Belgian F-104G, serial number FX67, is parked at RAF Woodbridge in England during Tiger Meet 69 on August 7, 1969. It was part of the 31st "Tiger" Squadron of the 10th Wing, based at Klein Brogel. This squadron's F-104Gs specialized in tactical-strike missions.

Belgian air force F-104G, serial number FX52, of the 1st Wing is parked on a hardstand at Upper Heyford, England, in June 1969. The Belgians assigned serial numbers FX01 to FX100 to their F-104Gs. Unlike German Luftwaffe F-104Gs, with straight demarcation between the upper and lower camouflage colors, the Belgians tended to use wavy demarcations on their camouflage. The 1st Fighter Wing was based at Beauvechain in Belgium.

Aeronautica Militare Italiana (AMI; Italian air force) F-104G, serial number MM6609, bears the rearing-horse insignia of 4° Stormo on its tail as well as the red, white, and green roundel of the Italian air force on its wings and fuselage. AMI received 114 F-104Gs in the early 1960s. These Starfighters were produced in Italy by Fiat, which also made F-104Gs for Germany and the Netherlands. Initially these F-104Gs were assigned to 4° Stormo (4th Wing) in 1963. Italy kept its Starfighters in service until the force transitioned to the Tornado in 1983.

An F-104G assigned to 6° Stormo, 154° Gruppo, is parked on a hardstand at Ghedi Air Force Base in Italy on October 16, 1972. The insignia of 6° Stormo is on the tail and features the likeness of a red devil. Bilingual English and Italian markings are stenciled on the aircraft, such as the "RESCUE/ SALVATAGGIO" instructional sticker and the "HANDS OFF BEFORE GROUNDING / ELECTRICAL SHOCK DANGER" on the edge of the antiglare panel to the front of the windscreen.

F-104G, AMI serial number MM6456, visits RAF Woodbridge on August 7, 1969. This Starfighter served with 53° Stormo, 21° Gruppo, stationed at Cameri Air Force Base. On the tail is the insignia of 53° Stormo, which features a vertical scimitar on a white rectangle with a letter A at the upper left and an inverted A at the bottom right. Italian air force Starfighters featured the Stormo number—53 in this case—as a fuselage prefix number. The other number is the individual aircraft number.

This Greek F-104G of 335 Mira, formerly USAF serial 61-2609, is serviced at Tanagra Air Base in June 1970. Greece also fielded the Starfighter. The Elliniki Vassiliki Aeroporia (Royal Hellenic Air Force) received its first thirty-five F-104Gs, built by Canadair, in 1964. Ten more Lockheed-built F-104Gs followed. These Starfighters were initially assigned to 335 "Tiger" Mira (Squadron), 114 Pterix (Wing), at Tanagra Air Base. Subsequently, more F-104Gs were assigned to 336 "Olympus" Mira, 116 Pterix, at Araxos Air Base.

To commemorate the retirement of the F-104Gs from 336 Mira of the Royal Hellenic Air Force in the early 1990s, the unit decorated a F-104G with a special paint scheme. A large, black eagle was painted on the fuselage against a backdrop of Mount Olympus and a bluish sky on the forward part of the fuselage and on the vertical tail. The number 7151 was painted in white on the rear part of the eagle. On the tail is the blue, white, and blue fin flash of the Royal Hellenic Air Force.

Turkish F-104G 22344 served with the 4th Wing, based at Mürted Air Base (now Akıncı AB), Turkey, in June 1970. The Türk Hava Kuvvetleri (Turkish air force) was one of the NATO air forces to be equipped with the F-104G. The Turkish air force received thirty-two F-104G Starfighters produced by Lockheed and Canadair in May 1963. The Turks received nine more F-104Gs in 1972. From 1980 until 1995, they received large numbers of F-104Gs from other air forces. Turkey ultimately operated or salvaged 400 Starfighters of various models.

F-104G, construction number 683D-7022, was assembled by Messerschmitt-Manching in 1962, using parts supplied by Lockheed. After serving with the Luftwaffe, the plane was retired from active service in January 1977; it continued to serve as an instructional airframe until the early 1980s. Following restoration work, this F-104G was delivered to the Deutsches Museum, in Munich, in March 1984, where it has remained on display. In April 2016, the aircraft was stored at Flugwerft Schleissheim, near Munich, while renovations were being performed at the Deutsches Museum. *Massimo Foti*

F-104F BB+362, former US serial number 59-4996, construction number 5049 of WaSLw 10 (Waffenschule der Luftwaffe) is prepped for take of at Jever AB, Federal Republic of Germany, in the late 1960s. This aircraft has been preserved and is on display in Munich. *Hans-Heiri Stapfer*

CHAPTER 7
NASA Gets Its Own Starfighters: F-104N

NASA, and its preceding agency NACA, operated several Starfighters. The three F-104N (not to be confused with the NF-104A aerospace trainers) were the only examples produced by Lockheed specifically for the aeronautic agency.

The F-104N is essentially a demilitarized F-104G. The space and weight saved by the omission of weaponry and military hardware allowed the installation of test NASA-specific equipment.

Delivered between August and October 1963, the three aircraft initially carried NASA serial numbers 011, 012, and 013. F-104A 013 was involved in one of the most famous—and expensive—crashes in US military aviation history.

On June 8, 1966, F-104N 013 was one of five aircraft that participated in a photo and publicity flight of aircraft equipped with General Electric engines. As the photo session was concluding, NASA chief test pilot Joseph Walker, who flew F-104N 013, collided with XB-70A 62-0207. The collision caused the destruction of both aircraft and the deaths of Walker and Maj. Carl Cross, the XB-70 copilot.

Postcrash investigations indicate that the massive size of the XB-70A led to considerable difficulty on the part of Walker to judge distance and position. Vortices caused the F-104N's left horizontal stabilizer to contact the XB-70A right wingtip. The Starfighter pitched over the bomber and tore off the Valkyrie's vertical stabilizers.

Subsequently, the other two F-104Ns were renumbered 811 and 812 and continued to fly for NASA until the mid-1980s, when both were retired.

All three Lockheed-constructed F-104N Starfighters fly in formation. The F-104Ns were built for NASA to use as supersonic chase planes. The planes were based on the F-104G and had all weapons systems removed to make room for equipment particular to NASA requirements. Initially, the F-104Ns were numbered 011, 012, and 013. F-104N 013 was lost in a midair collision with the second North American XB-70A Valkyrie on June 8, 1966. The collision resulted in the death of the F-104N pilot Joseph "Joe" A. Walker. The two surviving F-104Ns later were assigned civilian registrations N811NA and N812NA. *NASA*

F-104N 812 soars against a clear, blue sky. The plane had yellow-and-red decorative work on the tail, forward fuselage, and wings. The front of the inlet and the shock cone were matte black. *NASA*

NASA F-104N number 013 (to the immediate right of the XB-70 Valkyrie bomber) and several USAF fighter and trainer planes fly in formation with the bomber for some publicity photographs during the test of the second XB-70 Valkyrie over Southern California on June 8, 1966.

As captured on film seconds after the F-104N collided with the XB-70, the Starfighter explodes in a ball of fire. The damage to the empennage of the XB-70 (*lower plane to the left*) is visible. F-104N pilot Joe Walker was killed. The pilot of the XB-70 survived but the copilot died.

A NASA Starfighter tests insulation tiles to be used on the space shuttle. Starfighters were used in the 1980s and early 1990s for a variety of test projects related to the space shuttle. These materials were attached to a centerline pylon. *NASA*

The last US government operator of the F-104 was the National Aeronautics and Space Administration (NASA). NASA began to operate the F-104 at the Dryden Research Center at Edwards Air Force Base in California in August 1956. No fewer than eleven F-104s served the administration for a period of thirty-eight years, until the final F-104 flight in February 1994. Among the administration's fleet of Starfighters were three specially produced F-104N aircraft.

Among NASA's first uses for the F-104 was to train pilots for the X-15 rocket plane, which explored the edge of space. Other uses of NASA Starfighters included tests of thermal tiles and reaction control systems comparable to those used on spacecraft. Not surprisingly, privately owned F-104s are the aircraft of choice for a private firm that plans to air-launch small commercial satellites into space in 2023.

CHAPTER 8
The Canadian Starfighter: CF-104

In the late 1950s, the Royal Canadian Air Force sought a nuclear-strike fighter. After various options were considered, the Canadians announced the selection of the F-104 for this role on July 2, 1959. However, they wanted a Canadian-built aircraft outfitted to their specific requirements. Subsequently, a licensing agreement was reached with Lockheed for the production of Starfighters by Canadair in Montreal. An additional licensing agreement permitted the production of the J79-OEL-7 engine by Orenda Engines Limited in Ontario.

The Canadian-produced aircraft, designated the CF-104, was similar to the F-104G. However, it was tailored to the nuclear-strike role. As delivered, the aircraft were not fitted with the 20 mm M61 cannon typical of Starfighters. Instead, tanks for an additional 1,000 pounds of fuel filled the vacated space. The aircraft were also equipped with air-to-ground R-24A NASARR fire control equipment.

One US-built F-104A (USAF 56-0770, later RCAF 12700, finally RCAF 104700) was supplied to Canadair for use as a pattern for production. Canadair completed their first CF-104 in the spring of 1961. The first aircraft example, RCAF 12701, was airlifted to Palmdale, California, for flight testing. The initial flight occurred on May 26, 1961. A similar process was used with the second aircraft, serial number 12702. The next two CF-104s, 12703 and 12704, made their first flights in Montreal on August 14, 1961. The 200th and final CF-104 was completed on September 4, 1963. In 1970 the force shifted from nuclear strike to ground attack, and the M61 cannon was installed, along with twin bomb ejector rack carriers and rocket launchers. The last CF-104 was retired February 28, 1986.

Three CF-104s fly in formation with three US Navy F-4N Phantom IIs of VF-201 in 1976. The CF-104s have a mix of natural-metal finish, white wings, and red horizontal stabilizer. The Canadian firm Canadair produced 200 CF-104 Starfighters, based on the F-104G. *National Museum of Naval Aviation*

Canadair CF-104, Royal Canadian Air Force (RCAF) serial number 12797, displays the Canadian Red Ensign on the tail. Canada's national flag, known as the Red Ensign, featured the British Union Jack until 1965, when that flag was replaced by the more familiar modern flag that features a red maple leaf against a white square on a red field.

A Canadair CF-104 of the RCAF cruises above the clouds. On the tail is RCAF serial number 12797. The last three digits are inscribed near the front of the fuselage, to the rear of the RCAF roundel, which is blue and white with a red maple leaf in the center.

The new Canadian maple-leaf flag authorized in 1965 is on the tail of CF-104 12842. The CF-104 omitted the M61 20 mm cannon in favor of increased internal fuel tanks, with an additional capacity of approximately 122 gallons.

Royal Canadian Air Force CF-104, serial number 12750, bears a polished natural-metal finish. The edge of the inlet and the shock cone are painted a dark color. The RCAF serial number is on the vertical tail below the pre-1965 Canadian Red Ensign.

Royal Canadian Air Force CF-104, serial number 12797, flies in formation with two other Canadian aircraft of the 1950s. From left to right are the CF-104, an Avro Canada CF-100 Canuck fighter/interceptor, and a Canadair Sabre fighter. The CF-104 became the Canadair Sabre replacement in 1962.

Tiger-stripe-painted CF-104 12833, 439 Squadron, Canadian Armed Forces (CAF), is at RAF Woodbridge in England on August 7, 1969. The "CAF" markings dated to 1968, when the Canadian Army, Royal Canadian Air Force, and Royal Canadian Navy were united as the Canadian Armed Forces.

CF-104D, serial number 12655, of 439 Squadron stands ready. The CF-104D was a two-seat Starfighter built by Lockheed for the Canadians. The CF-104D lacked the M61 20 mm cannon. The plane displays a modern national flag on its tail.

CHAPTER 9

Built in Japan: F-104J

In late 1960, the Japanese Air Self-Defense Force (JASDF) selected the F-104 to replace the F-86F Sabrejet and become the nation's next interceptor. Agreements were reached with Lockheed and General Electric to license production of the aircraft and engine by Mitsubishi Heavy Industries and Ishikawajima-Harima, respectively.

The JASDF F-104s were armed with a 20 mm M61A1 cannon and four AIM-9 Sidewinder air-to-air missiles—two mounted underwing and two carried on a rack on the fuselage centerline. The aircraft were equipped with an Autonetics North American Search and Ranging Radar (NASARR) F15J-31 fire control system optimized for the air-to-air mode.

The very first F-104J built was produced totally by Lockheed in Burbank and made its initial flight on June 30, 1961. After testing, it was disassembled and shipped to Japan, where it was reassembled and again took to the air on March 8, 1962. Similarly, the second and third F-104Js were built in the US, dismantled, and shipped to Japan. The next seventeen F-104J aircraft were built on the Lockwood assembly line and shipped to Mitsubishi as kits, where they were put together. Twenty two-seat F-104DJ trainers were also sent as kits to Mitsubishi. Subsequent F-104Js were built completely in Japan by Mitsubishi.

The JASDF was equipped with twenty F-104DJ and 210 F-104J Starfighters in total. These were assigned to seven squadrons. The JASDF began to phase out the Starfighter in favor of F-15 Eagles from December 1981. The last F-104J retired in March 1986. During its service life, thirty-six JASDF Starfighters were written off as a result of accidents.

F-104J, serial number 36-8541, returns to Kwangju Air Base in South Korea after it participated in a "Cape North" exercise on May 1, 1982. After the first twenty Lockheed-built aircraft, Mitsubishi started licensed production of the F-104J Starfighter variant in Japan in March 1965. *USAF*

JADSF F-104J, serial number 26-8501, deploys its air brakes during a flight. The number 501 on the fuselage represents the last three digits of the JADSF serial number. It was assigned to the first F-104J, which was one of three manufactured entirely by Lockheed.

A towed target for aerial gunnery practice is carried under the left wing of JASDF F-104J, serial number 36-8550. The insignia of the 203rd Squadron is on the vertical tail. The insignia features a panda bear with two red stars and stylized red lightning flashes. *USAF*

F-104J, JASDF, serial number 46-8577, is manned at Hyakuri Air Base, in Japan, in 1974. On the vertical tail is the insignia of the 206th Squadron. The insignia features a red-and-white plum blossom superimposed on a blue stylized "7." The plum blossom symbolizes Kairaku Park in Mito, Ibaraki Prefecture, while the "7" symbolizes the 7th Air Wing.

CHAPTER 10
The Ultimate Starfighter: F-104S

The final and the most potent version of the Starfighter to see military service was the F-104S. The pilot of what would become the F-104S was created by Lockheed through modification of RF-104G serial number 64-2624. The modified aircraft first flew in December 1966. Subsequently, Lockheed was awarded a contract from the Italian government to modify Fiat-built F-104G MM6658 and F-104G MM6660 to serve as prototypes.

Production F-104S aircraft were built by Fiat from December 1968 through March 1979, most for service with Aeronautica Militare Italiana (AMI).

The F-104S was the result of a 1965 All-Weather Interceptor design competition held by the Italian air force. The F-104S was a further development of the F-104G and featured a more powerful J79-GE-19 engine, additional external stores strongpoints, and NASARR R21-G/H radar to work in conjunction with radar-guided missiles. The F-104S lacked the internal M61A1 20 mm cannon found on its predecessor because the internal space was needed for avionics and fuel. Two additional ventral fins were added; these also serve as the most readily visible characteristic of the type.

Aeronautica Militare Italiana (AMI) initially ordered 165 F-104S aircraft from Fiat. The first Fiat-built F-104S flew on December 30, 1968. The type entered active service with the 22° (Interceptor) Gruppo in June 1969. A further forty of the type were added to the order shortly thereafter for the Italian air force.

Turkey made clear its intent join the ranks of F-104S operations in October 1974, when it ordered forty examples of the advanced Starfighter.

The last F-104S was completed in March 1979. It marked the end of Starfighter production worldwide.

The F-104S was developed for the Aeronautica Militare Italiana (Italian air force) and first flew in December 1966. Two hundred were later delivered to the Italian air force, and a further forty for Turkey. The landing gear is extended, and the characteristic left ventral fin of the F-104S is visible on a Starfighter marked 5-41. It served with 5° Stormo, 102° Gruppo, Aeronautica Militare Italiana. The tail insignia has a depiction of Diana the Huntress within a circle.

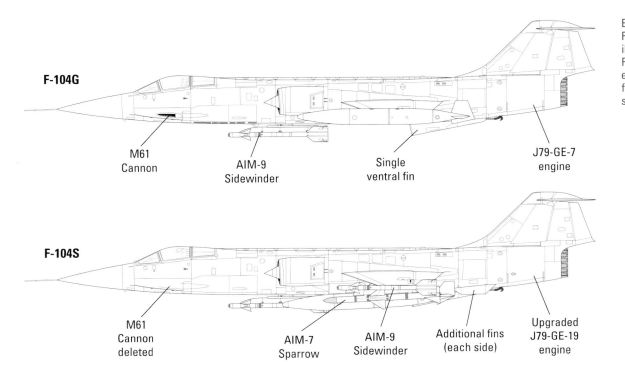

F-104G

M61 Cannon

AIM-9 Sidewinder

Single ventral fin

J79-GE-7 engine

Exterior differences between the F-104G and the F-104S are illustrated in these diagrams. The F-104S omitted the M61 gun and eliminated the single ventral fin in favor of a small ventral fin to each side of the fuselage's centerline.

F-104S

M61 Cannon deleted

AIM-7 Sparrow

AIM-9 Sidewinder

Additional fins (each side)

Upgraded J79-GE-19 engine

The Turkish air force acquired the F-104S from Italy and assigned it to 191 Squadron, based at Balıkesir in Turkey, in 1993. The F-104S was an improved version of the F-104G, with the more powerful J79-GE-19 engine and the North American Search and Ranging Radar (NASARR) R21-G/H radar. The new radar gave the Starfighter the capability to fire radar-guided missiles as well as a contour/ground-mapping and terrain-avoidance capability. The Turkish red, white, and red roundel is on the inlet, while the national insignia is on the tail.

A pair of Italian air force F-104S Starfighters along with a Turkish C-160 and a 36th TFW USAF F-15C occupy part of the ramp at Bitburg Air Force Base in Germany in April 1988. The Starfighters carry the red, white, and green roundels of the Italian air force on the fuselage and wings. F-104S aircraft could fire the AIM-9 Sidewinder and AIM-7 Sparrow missiles. *USAF*

Lockheed designed the F-104 Starfighter interceptor aircraft in the early 1950s to fly as high and fast as possible. This plane outperformed virtually all of its contemporaries. It served not only in the US Air Force but in the air forces of several allied countries as well. The Italian air force was the last to fly the F-104 operationally. Those aircraft, the F-104Ss, represented the ultimate development of the Starfighter and, fittingly, the last Starfighters in military service and were not retired until October 2004. Italy retired the F-104S in 2004—fifty years after the first flight of the prototype XF-104.